*according
to whiskey*

Also by Tom House

Inside These Walls (independently-released cassette)

Raw Bone (Audio CD of poetry readings)

The Neighborhood Is Changing (Checkered Past Records)

This White Man's Burden (Checkered Past Records)

'Til You've Seen Mine (Catamount Records)

Jesus Doesn't Live Here Anymore (Catamount Records)

Long Time Home From Here (Catamount Records)

the world according to whiskey

∼ poems by ∼
tom house

court street press
montgomery

Court Street Press
P.O. Box 1588
Montgomery, AL 36102

Copyright © 2003 by Tom House
All rights reserved under International and Pan-American Copyright Conventions.
Published in the United States by Court Street Press, a division of NewSouth, Inc.,
Montgomery, Alabama.

Library of Congress Cataloging-in-Publication Data

House, Tom.

The world according to whiskey : poems / by Tom House.

p. cm.

ISBN 1-58838-132-3

I. Title.

PS3608.O864W67 2003

811'.6--dc21

2003007254

ISBN 1-58838-132-3

Printed in the United States of America

contents

grinning through the teeth

for the record / 11
particulars / 13
a synopsis / 14
the backyard hoop / 16
mary ann ashworth / 18
the awkward age / 20
looking for his mama in a bar / 21
the city after / 23
where it's gone / 25
art? / 26
virginia reels / 27
roughing it / 28
& the mountain moved / 30
genius / 32
mother and son / 34
this year's cartoons / 36
sunday the thoughts come from miles around / 38
kicking off fan fair week / 40
saturday morning after / 42
west durham sundays / 43
the auction block / 44
delia / 45
the porno myth / 47
linda's trick / 49
drunk man stealing wife from himself / 51

the welder / 53
pilgrim escapes / 55
the holy primitive / 57
back room blood / 58
laying it low / 60
jewels / 61
the day the war began / 63
taking a vacation / 65
the getaway / 67
a story from the new south / 69
a suitcase for her thoughts / 71
the marriage / 72
heathen arms / 73
my penis / 75
to the bitter end / 76

perspectives

post modern graffiti / 81
the hank williams' memorial myth / 83
on the puppy dog news hour channel 4 / 85
that tunnel america / 87
going commercial / 89
watching the cable christians
—the gaudiest show in town / 91
whose business is sin? / 93
big dick dances / 95
all the raggedy-ass politics / 97
the change-your-attitude hour at the mississippi whiskers / 99
marlboro mama / 101
what is it? / 102
home / 103
the exhibitionist primps / 104

bug game / 105
blessed / 106
the performer grows older / 108
the bus home from nashville / 110
politics & poetry / 112
the outlaw / 114
spit-rap / 115

the world according to whiskey

the world according to whiskey / 119
brooding / 120
the masochist's solution / 122
jud dealt / 123
a ruthless coward and a mean drunk's what the judge said / 125
her handicap fetish / 126
cockroaches / 128
suicide at the school / 129
came to/wrote this / 131
skybrain and his pornography / 132
another psych major earns her spurs / 133
how it happened / 135
cause of death: pneumonia / 137
and i never ever really liked much about nothing / 139
the garbo game / 141
anima / 143
a modern romance / 145
tequila's gambit / 147
ms prissy / 148
small sacrifice / 150
the bondage model / 152
the live peep-show / 154
filling out the report / 156

i drop in the turf last friday night / 158
the bust / 160
the survival-reality game / 162
i make friends everywhere i go / 164
the outlaw legend/how it dies / 165
connie learns the tricks / 169
i ain't retarded but. . . / 171
cassie cops a feeling / 173
scars so quiet / 175
harry suggs / 176
the white man / 178
politics & pornography / 179
this porno shop / 182
ted bundy's mother / 183
good kids / 184
repast / 186
the boll weevil blues / 188

acknowledgments / 189

*grinning
through
the teeth*

for the record

are you a poet?

do you hang out
with other poets?

do you drink a lot?
or do other drugs?

do you submit to small press magazines?
(do you actually read them?)

are you happy?

would you consider yourself
introverted
extroverted
bohemian
well-adjusted
slumming
or what?

do you have many friends?
any friends?

is there any
overall design to
what you are
trying to do?

are you succeeding?
how long
will you
last?

particulars

some poets marry
sentiment to sadness

raise noise to the level
of orphans in an arena

some find love
in a pat on the back

some smash windows
some mirrors

a few claw their way home

(now and again
a good one learns
laughter)

most keep score
details to particulars
ways to win influence

beyond me now
i'll keep it blatant

i'd sing in a whorehouse

sign my name to
damn near anything

a synopsis

i was born normal
and grew up
bent

but ok

went to college
and crazy

but survived
like everyone else

we woke up drunk
all the time
and came here

to figure it out

our lives became
conclusions

we learned
to entertain
ourselves

i blacked out
into marriage
woke up

walked some streets

stared in
some windows

i confess
i never made
much money
at nothing

(my motives were
mostly just
beyond me

and i was
too easily
distracted)

we all did
what we could

i found
private ways
to prosper

the backyard hoop

he was 33
and crippled
had jumped
into the river
cracked his spine
on the rocks when he
was 17 his mother
took care of him
sat him up in front
of the window
two houses up
from where i
shot baskets
in the backyard
by the hour
all through
my high school
days somewhat
the loner
dissatisfied
with everything
but twirling
that basketball
with either hand
into the basket
from anywhere
driving hard and
stopping fast

and being
left alone
and i'd pass
his window close
and he'd just
turn his eyes
aside and never
said a word or
answered once or twice
i spoke to him
so i said
what the hell
ignored him
faked left
then right
leaping high
and concentrating
hit the shot
and won the game
over and over
(and the roar
of the crowd in
his silence)
the same last—
second fantasies
all them hot
and hateful
summer days

mary ann ashworth

we slept
in the middle of
a soft sand road

out of the way

landscaped lots
and an unsold brick
home or two

lots of high weeds
thick woods

she was 19 or so
and i was 16
first time i
ever drank beer
and on

a hot summer night
we spread a blanket
and did it
in the road

her on top
me looking up
at a multiple moon
the wind blowing

sand and tears
in my eyes

mary ann ashworth

her father owned
the development
she drove her own jeep

and i swear to god
she just crawled
all over me

the awkward age

leaps of faith
not my style

i accept nothingness

pull in my sheets
become winter

open my mouth
and blizzards rage

crowds create their whims
and leave me out

i don't care
i don't need blood

to keep me warm
i build walls

close doors
disappear

looking for his mama in a bar

he jarred
his heart
screwed
tight

pressure-cooker throb
believed in

a woman wrote the bible
on his body

going home with anybody
(no purity
in passion)

behind closed doors
myth

cotton-sucking
morning after

what's the difference
pays the tab

he's got
the lonelies
in his loins

"god laughs at them
laugh at themselves"

she'd get drunk
and tell him

the city after

1.
eggs shells remain
shrapnel-splintered doors
punctured in the night
scars and gashes that rip
across sand and concrete

factory beams snap
as easily as toothpicks
(or backbones)
movie-set storefront pasteboards
run in the rain

the homes are frozen
explosions of timber
and the blackened grass
is sown with salt
the furnace blazes

bricks are strewn
across the artless earth
sirens whine in the early cold
the foghorn's belch is tasteless

2.
weeds slice sidewalk
sleeves into strips
flowers burst cement collars

each time bulging muscles flex
the split is more profound
the tear a little deeper

ivy climbs and strangles lampposts
wires hang low with purple moss
(agility becomes its own reward)
the sun sizzles in a puddle
crazed men prowl the streets for game
i burn in the heat of the glare

the wind is a long distance
i hear wires crackling
on dry leaves

where it's gone

my tongue spears litter
in a city park

my hands will not applaud
i pay to gather my souvenirs

the war has taxed me
until i am trash

there is no inspiration

daughters and sisters
soft-selling themselves
avoid my eyes
with morbid precision

i'm concern come
with a postmark

i smile with a distance
some call a limp

art?

who masters what?

technique/
delivery?

what's there to salvage?

saddled with apologies
or wet with self

at one with the cause
or locked out of the house

hopped up on our crutches
wide open as whores

want it all
all the time

we sing out or sit down
celebrate
or conspire

to master
to matter

inspire or explode
performing
ourselves
to perfection

virginia reels

the fiddler resins his bow
and cocks his leg

taut strings quiver

virginia's suggesting
too much and knows it

a flatpick rifles ticklish strings
a red bandana sucks the sweat
from the caller's forehead
gossip rises from the rafters

virginia skips from arm to arm
blushing beer and summer night
and will not listen
to the tired talk of farmers' wives

she feels the fire inside her

(the summer stars laughing)
and she's as hot and red
as a quick pinch of hell

gliding through the flames

the last note of the last song
the first note of the next one

roughing it

fire drowned

started raining
and you and me

arms bundled
stoned breath

in your face
and mine

hands melting
between your legs

lean-to branches
shivering

laughing lips
your tongue

driving stakes
in my ground

and we're zipped
up touching

licking
teasing

just inside you
storming

like hell now
i can't stop

smiling
feels so good

& the mountain moved

high winds
coming on like
ocean waves

building
from way off
gawky pines pitching

and whipping their topknots
bending low
like to snap
and i sit

on a log with
my whiskey and
my fire won't die

wind sparks dancing
off into the high grass
and the roar
swirls and swells

through
my hot head
like laughter
the sky slit
and lightning

rips through to
cold bone and a
crackling shudder

o whiskey lungs
i am holy flames
dancing in the dark eyes
of the lord

genius

let's eulogize Pound now
not for the excellence
of anything he might have done
(cause really who can tell)
but for his genius for paranoia
Rimbaud the same
Artaud
and Kafka
Nietzsche
Strindburg
Sexton
Plath

they were ahead

until later
they had to sit listen

(and there's
no room for
the timid
down here)

you hear the whispers

c'mon
c'mon

in the back of the bus
Hemingway
got a chainsaw
and a bottle

mother and son

"it's the best
we can do"

she confides
in her hand

"the dishes are done
the day ends

i suppose it could rain
it matters
less and less"

i shiver
(and the words
slip bubbles
through my teeth)

reply how i
survive
very well

"my days and nights
are to the point —"

from bath to bath
between my toes
behind my ears

i celebrate
for you

our tragedies barely qualify

tonight
i'll think fondly
of long ago

as i bounce off
the walls of my room
like an
echo

this year's cartoons

laughter in cans
graffiti and smear jobs

cellophane caricatures

birds of prey
and politicians

all of us after something

just the revolution
left us confused

bored and bankrupt

gluttons for slapstick
playing with ourselves

in our bashful cubicles

needing approval
and nowhere to find it

we are all nearly
strangers now
and prefer it that way

(in the dark

and don't bother)

this year's cartoons
are fat and move slow

there will be no
news following

you can trust
for awhile

sunday the thoughts come from miles around

frying chicken splits
spits blood
grease

stings my arm
the mushrooms sizzle
in butter
and I

stand sweating
over the hot stove
tripping my gourds
and gospel

music mulling over
my soul in the wine
gone sour to my head

blisters
pucker up

sunday sky
going down

pale onion lips
and stringbeans
wilting

memories

of baptist
summer evening
gatherings

radio on a rampage
foot-stompin'
negroes screeching
"doncha tell Jesus
what i done"

hotter'n hell
as i care to imagine
southern women
squatting
comparing

men and kitchens

kicking off fan fair week

he's still up there playing
country corner u s a
across from the hall of fame
in parking lot 90 degree sun

going for guinness book of records
the promoter's hustling anybody
the girlfriend's pissed

"why the fuck you ain't got a tent man?
he can't sing in the goddamn sun
are you out of your fucking mind?"

and the cat plays on
sweating
stops
lone tourist asks him why
he don't do some of the newer stuff

"just like the older stuff"
he answers
"more real to me

hank
johnny horton
lefty
the old guys
aw shit"

tourist walks off
ten minute break's up
and it's all for nothing
he knows that
no one stops for long
it's a joke

he picks up his guitar
but he knows

saturday morning after

waking with both
feet on the floor
to a half-filled
mason jar of beer
some paraphernalia
scribbled panic poems
a bowl of corn and lima beans
a cockroach crawling
its butter-greasy film
the window fan turning slowly
its dull dum-de-dum
my head with big
gaps missing
i sit up
the tv's on
i squint through
the smudged lens
of my twisted wire frames
it's the three stooges
the clock swears 7:15
i'm sweating dizzy
numb and nearly nauseous
spinning slightly
trying to find a finger
and something
to put it on

west durham sundays

black '51 chevy sprouting weeds in the yard
brown toad hopping the clay ground
(what's left of the grass)

and the porch swing squeaking
and the tarred street
shiny with greasy sun

rednecked stiff-jointed men
with leather pouch faces
packing their jaws
with snuff or tobacco

slicing away the hot afternoon
with the casual flick
of strong thick wrists

and the shavings
in piles at their feet

a deadpan sameness to their faces
and little wit for conversation

listening to the women
through the windows
swinging rocking
and waiting

the auction block

The evangelist
conquers Africa.

Jesus puts shoes
on the savages.

History books headline
an oldtime revival.

Christians come
to shop and save.

Jesus crawls back on
the cross on the clock.

There's a whole lot of
shaking going on.

Missionaries swallow
the offering plate.

Gospel voices
snake-dance
a continent.

delia

the quiet
like shades drawn over sound
is dark and yellow
candles flames lick lips
tease shadows
a propellor fan
turns slowly

delia fills up
her clothes with body
and her mind
with facts
shatters nerves
with touch
forgets her station
describes herself as if
she describes a lover's whims
i play deaf

wrap myself like a sheet
around her
the wind through the window
is warm with new rain
"she'll have
none of this shit"
she keeps
laughing and saying
her smile like the

moon on a garden
the smell of wet leaves
black earth
in my nostrils

her touch
like a shiver
in the dirty light
(the culmination of
mythology and
natural fact)
alive and crawling
a breathing nest
of tangled vines

the porno myth

1.
the daughter of darkness smiles
her bruised face like
a leaf in the storm

a predictable hybrid
she won't deny it

but explain with her fingers
how muscles can be tamed

the wind howls its opinions
trees collapse into splinters

and civilizations flourish
like greedy children
in her lap

2.
genius
chaos?
creation
their struggle

to outlast each other
outwit eternity

and justify their

meager moment

chaos climbs the pedestal
wraps her legs around his head

and rides the cyclone
senseless

3.
genius
(chained
raw

ejaculating
obscenities)
families drip down walls
puddles form in gardens

the daughter of darkness
bathes

linda's trick

linda like
some life she's
lost

smelly mattress
stale perfume

grabbing
all she's worth
and tugging

you like
something she
just found

a treasure or
a recipe

slippery with sweat
and righteous

her liquid tongue
turns up the gas

goes blue
with flames

and finds you

in her mouth
your blood
begins
to boil

drunk man stealing wife from himself

naked on a mule
in a mudslide

laughing on the pillow
of his brain

the last man
out the door

watches his life

mount a stallion
in a snowstorm

and ride it
with a brutal if

appropriate beauty
into the ground

candle in a bottle
through a tear

like the multiple exposure
of the glass in his hand

its reasons

for being there

her memory
like a bruise
on his palm

the welder

came home from
the war that
wasn't a war

a grim/grimy skeleton
with no use
for tittletat
or bullshit

twists them rubber-wrapped
coils around his hairy
wrists and hoists

his body
onto a spider beam
that sways above
the swirling mud

(flashing images
hot wet jungle

blood and guts
and good good drug)
pulls

the steel together
with veins bulging
he's straining

bitter strength
the rods in his hand
spit sneering
fluorescent arcs

(and everybody
shields their eyes)

he moves in grinning

like a surgeon
at a holiday feast

pilgrim escapes

envelopes like suitcases
address stickers reminders

of those moments
when the pilgrim slept
and someone tried
to call him home

between the jokes and the insults
the bloodline priorities
the nervous network panic

of interstates and alleys
windshield wipers like spiders
waking panicked

rain like rumors
he can't deny but still
his heart some swallowed breath

zipping bars his lips
superciliously

shudders   shivers some touch
he dreams could not be true

this poem about the sun rising
this time the interstate's

like hemp and duct tape

ribbons scarves
and handcuffs/chains
he blinks hard frantically
and promising

his life
somewhere else
right now

the holy primitive

brushing branches from my face
to the lazy twang of radio

i stroll naked through your wilderness

we fall and wrestle
we sweat and swim

holy men dance to clocks
at your feet

a world repents
not i

i come crawling through the thicket
bury my face in the bush and burn

salvation stalks your promises
wolves howl in the distance

i press my face against your window
and worship

back room blood

the guitars
crank it up

plucking taut   strung nerves
loudly
and we listen
find teeth
in violence
and
pull apart
still
clinging   fighting
to free ourselves
(tears blinking
eyes like nervous
neon lights)
sweat floods
the surface breaks
baptizing
sinners
burns and blurs
our vision
the gospel   groping
slippery
touch of bodies
as the radio blares
and the music has
rabbit feet   thumping

in the back rooms of
my filthy
little
heart

laying it low

morphine dissolves
the marrow in his bones

and all the pain from
the world he pursues

this poet receives
salvation on demand

rides a dead horse
into the desert

wears it like a napkin
to bed

the sun is a nipple
a doorbell to heaven

he praises veins with psalms
hydraulic syringes

pump fists into songs
inspired nonsense

steaming in the heat
of his hissing brain
laying it low
he calls it

his saddled tongue
standing at her door

jewels

tonight
is a plateau
a collaboration

insults rule
the hearth

i wait
like a slab of meat
for season
in the dark

and your touch
is so precise

metamorphosis
almost occurs

i almost
outlast my manhood
and spit my hymn
into the fire

my tongue
like a razor
in the rain
growing hotter
and redder

you crawl through
the smokehouse
on blistered knees

lunging for those
unshaven brats
who will fight you
all the way

fallen pilgrims
drunk with
your dream

strung out
like shiny jewels
on a desert

the day the war began

like comets falling
through powdered clouds
swirling bombs of white light
dropped through the haze
of a cronkite dusk
and splattered the horizon

you ran to the window
and drew me like eyes to an accident
from the safety of a silent screen
a guarded chair
a sweating can

birmingham
i thought aloud
watching the rain clouds primp
the sky suck in its belly
the sun gasping winking gone

an alley cat and her kittens
were chasing paper leaves
up and down the fire escape
fingers peeled curtains
and played on window spines
fear came calling in skeleton drag
long black robes like a judge's
wrapped around him

heaven split   we braced ourselves
the undigested roar of night planes
a headful of ideas (with parachutes)
falling like seeds from a ruptured heart
the fear itself the one thing
we could neither share nor avoid

and though we promised ourselves
other mornings fairer odds
i don't believe we ever thought
the sun was ours to share again

the last thing we saw
was the moon in splinters
a '57 cadillac crashed through
a storefront glass
a lake of phosphorescent light
and dragged the clouds
like curtains down behind it

taking a vacation

we sat there
leaning against concrete
picnic table overlooking
center hill lake
brook hollow cove
foggy night

looking like twilight
door into nowhere
and that's where i am
in and out nearly gone

leaping/diving
hurling fool self
into that swirling gray smoky
nothingness
and she don't know what's wrong with me
& i don't either

whether the pressure's me
or the world   or the lacking
mine/hers
i could sling up
the shit all night and she knows it
that wind's no mercy
like riots and headaches
hot and sticky
and i know

it ain't her

and she slides into the tent
and i pull on this joint hard
float away

the getaway

a christmas tree
wrapped with tinsel
facedown on the curbing

in the slow grip of freezing ground
the moon like chalk
through cashmere clouds

blue smoke
rising from your fingertips
you dump your ash in your saucer
watch it dissolve
in a ring of cold
black coffee

outside
two dogs prowl
through
the overturned garbage

you exhale wearily
the kitchen air dies
the night sky wrinkles

i'm bloated with beer now
i've had my say

you stand and leave

the room without speaking

i raise the window
stick my head into
the winter night

the cold air sponges my forehead
(you are drawing lines with your bath)

i stare long and hard
off at nothing

the christmas tree
shivering and laughing
in the quick wind
of escaping dog

a story from the new south

brittle stalks
dried weeds
hollow bones
sliced cleanly
below the knees
don't tell me   i know
i trudged her muddy fields
up to my ankles
i listened
as the crickets chirped
and i could see her outlined
darkness

waiting
quilted
quiet
night
her impatient legs
her expectant palms
rubbing together
it is neither   call
nor cry
young men challenge
the darkness
young men shining scarlet
their necks
straining with the effort

we come in from the fields
we remove ourselves from nature
we no longer even
grace the porch

a suitcase for her thoughts

one of them dry windy pieces
where none of the characters
care all that much
for the lines they're stuck with
spit out like dust
sitting hunched over cafe coffee
his eyes wandering
her splitting seams
when she breathes
and her wind like perfume
to him though he'd never think
to say so to her
she's laughing to herself swear to god
she can't make him out
and dense hell she's got
tomorrow on her mind
that sidewalk outside to anywhere
stirring and licking her plastic spoon
and him going on and on about some nothing
shit she's been thinking about dallas
and maybe even further

the marriage

i could talk about the shortcuts
embarrass us both

she needed a knight
and settled

i could tell you about the windmills
and the short breath

the ploughshare
the late fire

the harvest and the famine
i could tell it all

i rode a slow bus from the dakotas
with her scent in my clothes

i never forgot her

it was a long walk
to a dingy little station

heathen arms

sick of the sea
and the symbolic search
at the door of damascus
the end of a bottle

jabbing harpoon
into thick juicy blubber

on the edge of my knees
a runaway lust
always satisfied
with thin lips
teasing
tomorrow
relax

we have hours to sleep
before we test the plank
martyrs can't improvise
the script predicts itself
a lust that won't follow itself
into extinction is no lust
we faithless followers
sleep where we can
and god has no mind about it
(oceans
deserts
as you will)

personal distances
romantic frustrations
self-gratification
quick   and again
hate humbles all
and the christians can't laugh

as the room starts to swirl
don't fight it
ride it

one option
a drowning righteous soul
to be swallowed
in the sly embrace
of drunken
heathen arms

my penis

experiences no compulsions

to be an automobile
nor a boat

a football team
nor a checking account

it is grotesquely
less inhibited than i

and nearly as inconsistent

we try to concur
on what is tasteful

i exaggerate its excesses
it exaggerates mine

honesty between us
depends upon
the hour

to the bitter end

crushing
roaches
into pulp

chasing them
with my shoe
up and down
the walls

offering no
apologies

for the speckled
smears and bits
of chitin

the bodiless
twitching
antennae

my crazy laughter

(my tongue
thick and
sticky with
wine)

i fire up

a joint
and ride
the blur

(the room
already glazed
with smoke)

there is no
plan or purpose

to the poem
or the night

perspectives

post modern graffiti

how close are we getting
to the idea that art
no longer bound to church
or state
ideals or romance
has become the province
of misfits and ne'er do wells
who   unable to adapt
to life in the richest
most enlightened
and wonderful society
civilization has afforded
merely spread their discontent
negativity
and frustrated selves
for no other reason
beyond some infantile
striking out
or shouting down
majority —
programmed
utilitarian
sensibilities
how close are we getting
to the idea that art
should be "morally" correct
"spiritually" uplifting
"politically" right

not to mention
packaged properly
(the greatest meaning —
the largest audience)
how close are we to prosperity
looking freer than art
how close are we
to pissing it all
away

the hank williams' memorial myth

i walked off-stage
with ol' hank
and i never did   look back
the lights are bright
applause is loud
but proud ain't right
necessarily
and sometimes the guts
of the moment get
all twisted
and you've got to give more
expecting less
and if it ain't on
record or tape
or film   does that
mean it never happened
if someone important
you know
don't stamp it   his seal   say
yeah
this cat was pretty hot

naw   i walked off —
stage with ol' hank
that night
so drunk i could have
stumbled   but didn't
and wouldn't   and

surprising them all every turn   more'n
they ever could   or did   me   kept
step keeping it
hard beat lowdown
right there
kicking up   howling how
making it made sense   more'n
anything this moment
really might have meant
and no   i ain't saying
demons are gospel but
none of us are   sour-ass
sonuvabitches
can kiss mine   he laughed
then took aim   shot out
the spotlight

on the puppy dog news hour channel 4

tonight there's old hearts bleeding
misery of feebleness and agencies
protect us from ourselves
sonuvabitches
all of them overweight
and so comfortably sure of self
"one day we'll just walk in and find her dead"
about the old black woman husband cares for her
same squalor they've lived all their lives
and the disgust   the poverty   the roaches the filth
a little self-serving   the fine sensibilities
the social services representative
she'd prefer to break up the relationship
though one day somebody anywhere gonna just walk
in and find her dead what i'm thinking
their guilt or their god or their politics
or suffering humanity 12-step recompensation
trying to justify whatever theory
got to get out of people's lives
the old man is surly   he moves her
and feeds her
telling her to shut up   shut up
in an even voice   her constant
shrill complaining and he feeds her slowly
patiently as she stares at the camera
though now they can't get her to answer
a single question she looks at him
then back   that camera her hard eyes locked

a dying woman all these lights camera action
wants to know
where the fuck you been
all my life
and why are you here
now

that tunnel america

and tell them THEY
are the photogenic newscasters
who read the teleprompters
mindlessly/sincerely   convincing themselves
this story even more painful
than the last one
who are THEY?
they are the political choices
men who lead us   the options presented
we exercise our democratic rights of futility
and the advertising agencies and the pollsters
and the PEOPLE magazine
tell us why we are all so   alike
i am   aren't you?
you saw it   read it   felt it
understood it   bought it   did it
or didn't do it   (depending on which expert
this week endorses
or denounces it)

i sit hours   staring tv
seeing nothing but the flickering
shadows my eyes
and i'll pour down the wine
and the wickedness
chase my consciousness
quick shots
public showdowns

see what kind of humiliation
finally humbles me
maybe none
maybe all of them
the sun scares me pink (call it dawn/
call it monday/ call it off)
the hero cuts loose his bonds
with a sliver of mirror —
and maybe i'll just
crawl in there
behind him

going commercial

it's the trivialization
of damn nearly everything

polls/odds
each plan of action
subjected to instant
analysis/replay
all possible angles

you begin to feel
a little inhibited?

and the audience has seen it all before
will not be wowed   oh no
will sit there reminded
someone/something
seen or heard before
(and who really cares?)

the widest palm
the greenest buck
status-quo
adolescent claw

consume/consume
the sensational
simulation
of life

on a treadmill
the MEDIA
the CORPORATIONS
FAT CATS

— paranoia causes problems —
pace yourself
(here
have a hard-on
or a drink
turn on your tv
we're the best and the brightest
the richest
the toughest)

but would you go to war
for MOBIL OIL?
IBM? NBC?
(how would you
ever know?)

watching the cable christians
—the gaudiest show in town

bible-quoting
rifle-toting
christian soldiers
on the march
self-promoting
set their sights
on theirs by right
virtue born well-off
and white
and god's drunken power
the way they portray him
the way they worship
the way they pant
with that heathen rhythmic
mechanical surge
and the war clocks in
crusades & purges
everybody talking about
that greater glory
the polished greed
as testimony
in the twisted heart
where we can't pretend
the human peels the skin his need
points his weapon spilling seed
dribble down the corridors
corners of the mouths

the hustlers & the whores
the do-withouts understand
all the slamming doors mean
nothing's changing evermore
and your life's like
that pitiful orphan
in that movie saying
please sir i want some more
and all of us are saying it
deep down in our souls
this sonuvabitch is selling
salvation a small donation
there's more to us than history
or destiny controls
bleeding the turnips
and turn up their noses
the poor have so much more to give
and where we're taking the future
there ain't no soul to save
but if jesus hadn't risen
jesus hadn't risen
if jesus hadn't risen
he'd be turning
in his grave

whose business is sin?

whose business is sin?   let me think about it now
the profits the bosses carry as crosses
the chunky-cheeked priests
lily-white congregations
the cop on the street   organized crime
the judge and his friends   the whims of the time
nickels and dimes and who can afford justice good lord
the community's skin's too damn thin
say it again and you'd better believe it
you live in a crowd
you can't have too much insurance
and don't get too loud   keep your eyes to yourself
you get too out of line   you don't fit in anywhere
move along   keep the change   sort of thing

now you're talking 'bout sin
like it's something gonna end
you're gonna trade in your lust
for a full gut and trust a sanitized
subsidized version of getting it
cruising off the conveyor   ain't nobody sweating it

succeed as a need as a right as a creed
as your back starts to bend and your balls start to bleed

and you're still good for a laugh looking to find
something sounds like the truth
on the edge of it all   an ideal or a sorrow

    like the pulse of a mob   got you hung up the closet
       the scaffold the wall   fighting off demons
             you don't half recall
           and balanced so well
             you can't ever fall

  so look yourself in the eye see if handling why
    it would matter at all that you lived or you died
   can get next to you close to you like it's eternity
the last glimpse that you get before the eye finally blinks
and when it comes down to fact and your life is your past
   the answer you give when your god finally asks
            whose business is sin?
        why it's the devil's my friend
    and you're known by the company
               you keep

big dick dances

big dick dances
with his eyes zipped

and the world like a mob
all around him

his honor (the judge) jacking
jaws & prices

decides the odds of thickwitted men
against the guile
of desperate ones

whether this crisis
like so many others

can be blessed
& broken into miracles
(the proper corpse raised
from the appropriate grave

and the jury convinced
to hang itself
starve
or abstain

that justice might not lose face
& some kind of order be maintained)

— sex married to love
and tired men
told how to perform—

the judge (his honor) scratches
his dusty balls

the slot machine sighs
the trapdoor swallows

big dick dances
without benefit of partner

children chase his legend
down dead-end alleys
with sharp sticks

all the raggedy-ass politics

    where we gonna hide the landfill
    so white folks don't have to see it
    — white folks with money anyway
        voted the right way

    well   we can't have it here
       our beautiful facility
     for treating the alcoholic
    to a pretty penny's worth
       pleasant surroundings
     detox and some 12-step
  (and well sure   we deserve
what we pocketed   for the good
that we've done — we're 4 the family
      (like the tv channel)
    everybody get mindless
  clean   healthy   smile now
  ok   let's get that fucking
    landfill somewhere else)

      put it by the river
    never mind the water
    the people can afford it
    don't drink it anyway
we're talking years from now won't matter
     the styrofoam muzzles
     the throwaway people
     the chemical cancers

      crawling
    (the shine on
     the face of
       it all)

        hey!!
where we gonna hide the landfill
   government and business
  and they're nearly the same
consigned us to second-rate future
go along with the lackluster now
kind of hard simply toss a match
  and let it   burn baby burn

the change-your-attitude hour at the mississippi whiskers

and she's thin around the waist
and she walks with a sway
back to the bar takes a sling on her beer
putting em away   she's 40 45
but a robust flavor elegance
still alive and gonna have her say

now this character in the sports coat's alright
though he's slobbering a little
she don't deal that shit's what she's telling him
she's dripping all sarcasm and sex
and i ain't got time to figure
what happens next

i'm playing the happy hour
change your attitude
and i'm 27 or 8
and mine's basically crude
and i'm stomping and growling
up there on the stage
for two hours for ten dollars
supper and beer

and she don't think much of me
that's easy to see
and i don't much give a fuck
what she thinks about me

and when that finally gets through
she sort of gets intrigued
and i get back up there
the last set she's roaring
yelling out i'd take you home tie you up
i'd do things to you boy
and i'm pounding away some blues
and laughing like maybe
that would be alright too

and the character in the sports coat
he ain't figured shit out!

marlboro mama

she flew rages
warring
a woman's fears

paper dolls
and daddy daddy
nazi boot-stomp

(snap out of it
just when
she needs to)

put her face on
gertrude stein

dressed in tie
tails
and tuck it in

(just like a man)
grins

her favorite song
"walking the floor
over you. . ."

what is it?

what is it
the occasion
my madness

to be so arrested
in my soul
i twist

this slow foul wind
of doubt & indecision

& where my faith is eccentric
& where the sacraments seem silly

i can't witness
the truth i see
in the warm decomposing
of the body in the ground

& the rain that falls
& the spring & the winter
i was a part
of it all

home

home is where the
heart is

back when
you still had one

home is
where the part is

memorized to death

home is where you ran from/
ran to

home is what
you understand
is true

makes you
feel like
you

the exhibitionist primps

The moon spins on a bar stool.
Dogs curse their collars.

The exhibitionist serves his time
as preamble to hysteria.
Zippers keep him honest.

He's the rough draft of a tough guy;
the prize at the bottom of Pandora's box,
the original Beefcake Kid,

flexing his muscles
(raising his sights)

and there's no one bold
enough to remind him

that sometimes an audience
is the only friend
a naked man deserves.

bug game

alright
you are "born"
into one of any permutations

race/nationality/time slot
the last 43 years

rating power/
mobility/
other secondary characteristics

can be developed
as the game evolves

all have certain needs
some have others

there is no time limit
no particular object to this game

it is over when you "die"
afterward
a summation

seems like
it's worth it
or not

blessed

"amens"
ripped from roots
prayers
excuses
apologies

the tantrum can be pacified
all the time with anything

the final condition of freedom
to define and stomach itself

we bow to the weathervane
begging backbone and blessing

direction
meaning
purpose

stammer and almost
and can't quite
and so on

about rainbows
and fairy tales

and our father   who art
so mercifully

indifferent

give us faith
and keep us
occupied

the performer grows older

and he sniffed about

like a wild dog sniffing
at the hollow of
each passing clump of brush

the soles of his feet
wet from scraping concrete

a man of stature
condemned to travel corners
as naive as any child

crazy for the circuses
and midways mired in mud

and he drank to the promise
of the spotlight

pulsing blinking neon chains
held against a summer sky

facing only question marks
from such a dizzy distance

human voices swallowed to the
calliope's gulping reel

songs and pumpkins
dancing at midnight

and he cried
but that was only
a pearl in the wind

one sweating hand
catching the other

his voice like a wire
gone slack as he flexed
above the big top
his tears had soaked
the sawdust
he pawned the only watch
he'd ever owned

went home
and slept
on cotton
sheets

the bus home from nashville

my guitar went flat
on the bus home from nashville
after sixteen hours
went in its compartment
between a duffle bag and dryer
as i slept with my wine-skin
surrounded by soldiers
going home with permission
and woke up sweating
with a highway headache
and the re-run of the road
repeated through the night

morning added light to heat
the mountains blocked
the breeze behind us
heading east
into lunch and afternoon
a student in her teens
going home for a week-end
from a community business college
hopping from one small town
to another
and i sat behind the window
as the bus gulped down the miles

and my soul went flat
on that bus home from nashville

the strings that held it
attached to me
stretched dull/grew limp
i couldn't hold a tune
i strained and sighed and soured
as i counted the road signs
floating past tobacco fields
and grandchildren
tapping my toe
as if finally i had
heard my song
and understood
its rhythms

politics & poetry

suppose
censorship is
marketplace
access
resistance crushed
that compulsion to succeed
/the financial
illusion of freedom
the outrage recedes

suppose
your times insured
you had to say
the ridiculous
the concerns
the people listening
make sure
who hears what
access america
and you play their hand
you're such

a romance   and
revolutionary/   saxophones
say so
all about you
your voice
the wilderness

genius
the wind
howling wild
phantom
nowhere

the outlaw

the cowboy
is tan   lean
schizophrenic

he holds
his sixgun
one hand

his whiskey bottle
the other

he's singing
his one song
alone
campfires
glow in his eyes

his fingers
gallop
the horizon

spit-rap

spew   spew   spew
why am i so angry?
politics and poverty
personal doubts
and the nebulous
everything

poetry as private peek
David Rigsbee
once defined it as "a
slit across the throat
of time" freeze the film
get the details

i don't consider
poetry stands for nothing
but itself
poetry at all
problem with the conveyor belt
mentality tied to "making a living"
doing it —

the true poet is
not only putting out
"product"
he is using that effort
to structure whatever vision
whipped him up to the effort

in the first place
whatever sense of "lacking"
or confidant "abundance"
myth or mission
or personal obsession

the artist should get
to the end of the page intact
going for greatness
anything you say may
be used against you

some poets just stride
right through the shit
some sit home
scribbling
waiting

the world according to whiskey

the world according to whiskey

that whiskey
you don't fuck
with brother
it leave you
whistling the
other side
of the mirror
& your eyes
get so dark
you don't even
know it

stay away from that
strong need
you tickertape
down the alley
a garbage can guru
they knock out
your teeth then
they stomp you
just to show you

brooding

i practiced
being alone
tonight

touched myself
until i tired

puffed an anchor
around my soul

turned out
the lights.
and sat there

fat with self
and practiced

being lost
tonight
the dark
the roar
of oceans
inside me

stumbling
on the rocks

breathing my name

watching my chest

rise and sink
with the tide

over and over
and over
again

the masochist's solution

impatience is a virtue
and afterthought
a luxury

we ritualize more than
celebrate out lives

pulling off   what we do
through bluff or blunder
mostly

teasing ourselves
with random mirrors
and quick solutions

we choose from what
we'll comprehend

(what i can't do

i never wanted to
really . . .)

the convenience of our pain

we eventually choose
to enjoy it

jud dealt

his junk
a hotdog joint

over on roxboro rd
nobody ate there
grease had bug wings

floating in it
he sold soft drinks and candy
to the neighborhood kids

and four dollar bags
get two of us off til
we can't hardly walk

let us hit up back there
in the bathroom
plenty of times

jud's 54
taking him 20-30 minutes
find him a vein
you're alright —
he's telling me
bobbing his head
dancing bubble

still grinning

you know
i been a junky
this town since '47

wasn't 'til you white
kids came along cops
knew about niggers
and drugs
at all

a ruthless coward and a mean drunk's what the judge said

dirty harry drunken bully county sheriff
shooting flies off the ceiling in the jail with a
shotgun and he threatened to murder
a prisoner once

been caught with a stolen sheep in missouri
motel room and picked off tamed ducks at the
highway patrol station pond with his .22

some that sort of liked him lots more were afraid
rural area he was authority
kind of a legend
him and his daddy

went crazy was working this transient as a
slave on his farm beat his wife with a hose he
swears he just don't remember (about the time
he was on the network news catching that prison
escapee with the pistol to his head push his face
back in the mud and commentator in new york
called him a hero)

her handicap fetish

marcie used
to strap
her ankles
her knees
the metal
brace her
feet pinched
her mother's
feet much
smaller

marcie would
tremble her reflection
she'd shuffle
from the back door
to the front room
stand behind
drawn curtains
playing
the tapes
her head
she remembers
her mother's
eyes
the lines
the lips

the door kicked open

    the sun going down
       the shadows
         the men
      she's twisting
        her torso
        reaching
        blocking
        the fear
      like snakes
    chopped in two
        don't die

  she hears the hiss
         voices
     she can't rise
     she can't cry
   like the leather
   and the metal
    lock her legs
     and don't
         give

cockroaches

lick the grease
from the butter
knife skimming
puddles silly
bastards late at
night crawling
walls laughing
at you surviving
350 million years
and who knows
how many strong
no brain just a
razor react reproduce
and run attitude
live on what you
got not choosy
take over the world
while you sit there
drinking beer
watching tv

suicide at the school

towel
strip
twisted

like a thick
grip on throat

sprinkler
system
nearly
bent to the floor
(his big toe
bulging

through
tennis shoe
canvas)

t's and blues
and whatever else
all the students knew

knew
all
along
he came home
from a week-end

someone tried to
love him
or buy him

or something
("i was fucked up
man...")

just remember
he kept asking

someone tell him
what he missed

the fan dries my eyeballs
soft contacts constrict
i sit stoned/drunk
who knows how long

came to/wrote this

blew off the '60s
smoking pot slows it all down
to right now
no good getting tongue-tied
a good percentage idealism
has to be impractical
and there's some of the charm
and the rest nostalgia

like there's a door says bring it on
and all reason fails us
some nerve won't serve

everybody covering ass
got to maintain the cool
stay strong in the eye
i start the fire in the basement
with a stack of old rolling stones
this rock and roll bullshit
is yesterday

skybrain and his pornography

Skybrain sleeps at the foot of the page
"is there evil?" he asks
as pathetically as Job

"most likely not"
as she straps him in

pain is a purpose amid this pandemonium
any little touch will keep him going

Skybrain squeezes his sponge
a transparent woman
drowns in his mirror

she wraps herself in searchlights
that cling oily and shiny as latex

Skybrain tears off his coupon
and dives into debt

on her scent
to the edge of his wits

humbling himself
turns the page in a hurry —

holds his swollen gift
in lonely
outstretched
hand

another psych major earns her spurs

Margy took her degree from Duke
and her hard-luck
laugh it off humanity

too seriously
for waiting tables
answering phones
or missionary work
(wife position)

took a job
"The Magic Touch"
worked her way up
smiling
hustling
lay it on thick
open up wide

don't matter
who's stroking it
takes it out of their hands

coming home
5:30   6 in the morning
Michael   her old man
can't take it no more
"Crawl up it" she tells him
peeling her spandex

drawing her bath

night after night
men with their pants down
her attitude got hard
ain't no one tough enough
to touch her now

how it happened

was early august
we'd been separated
since april still
saying we'd get back
together believing
it less and less
and i dropped over
should have been
working wasn't
i was hungover
driving around
mid-afternoon
walked on in
her bedroom door
locked and blood
charging the air
a growling "what the
fuck you want?"
"to speak with my
goddamned wife" reply
and she came out
in her housecoat
and couldn't look
at me tears in eyes
crying she was sorry
and i had no idea
if she meant she
was sorry i had

come upon her
or sorry we had
come to this
"it don't matter"
i shrugged
and suddenly
it didn't

cause of death: pneumonia

he passed out
4:30   5 in the morning
after hours cussing
and shouting this and
slinging that
and slapping at her
punching her telling her
two boys to get their fucking
asses back to bed or he'd
by god show them the way
and she sat there
a long time thinking
'bout it she'd
planned and plotted
and overcoming
everything she'd
ever been or feared
slipped the handcuffs
on his wrists and
wired them to the bedframe
cut off his britches
and lashed him
to the mattress
and when he woke she
was leaning there on
the edge with the
bucket in her hand
and he's soaking in

sheets and cold water
she reaches over
slaps him again and
again and when she stops
penetrating eyes
he's never seen before
she turns on the fan
starts to laugh
starts to shiver

and i never ever really liked much about nothing

my name is mark howard i'm a lefty
and i started on the state high school team
my sophomore year i got in a fight
and i sat on the bench til i figured that one out

then i learned to shoot pool
and i was slicker'n grease
an eye like a cobra
and a style for awhile
i took up with this woman
used to hang out in her high heels
and her nostrils flaring
like emergencies
she go rushing
the chemicals her head
crushed against
a telephone pole
it was snowing
and she was wasted

and i got into the needles
and i got into the rituals
the staring off dead
little corners of life

smoked so much i got lost
and sipping the red wine

pop some speed   keep it going
and he's just the first guy that we saw
that's all i'd never seen him before
me and billy patterson
on our last legs home
a motherfuckin jogger
you know what i mean
and i wasn't sure i was going to shoot
it weren't nothing personal
i just decided to kill
the next person we met
that's all

the garbo game

she sits
blue haze against
the headboard
sheets wrapped
around

eyes so
he can't see
the passion
long gone
she owns her bed
"all a woman
really needs"
she curls
and spits
it hoping
just maybe

but no
there's no
reaction
she jabs
the cigarette
out and kicking
at him
slings the
ashtray
coming nowhere

close

he's left
her out   and
dirty   aching
wants to hurt him
crawl inside
and make him
want her
make him
need her
tell him
no

anima

there's a woman
inside me
playing with herself

dips her tongue
the vinegar
and dances away

stuffs her bra
with ballots
hangs me in her closet

the man i think i am

survives the politics
and busy work

goes diving for the moon

this woman
deep inside me

like a fullness
of purpose
or expression

threatened
or embarrassed

in my honor

fuck 'em   she laughs
turning herself inside out

where no one else
can find me

and we dream
cheek to cheek
to the radio

all night
long

a modern romance

a woman
painted a mouth
on her lies
a man made
too much
of the money
defined him
he thinks
he controls
how pretty
the mouth speaks
so well of him
his prowess
his virtues
accomplishments
a man learns
his lies loudly
he loves
her red lips
locked around
his cock her eyes
demonstrably
devout   she
accepts her femininity
he believes in
himself and
the way things are
when he kisses her

he crushes her to him
and when he leaves
he slams the door
and when he's here
he's her everything
and when he's gone
he's absolutely
nothing

tequila's gambit

it's the sober mind suffers scrutiny
tequila slams doors
ignores

headlines
conclusions
odors and gossip

screws tighten guts
to nearly in focus

tequila sucks in
his nuts and
continues

charity cripples us all
"i'm just like you"
pound the hearts in the dark

tequila won't hear it

sacrificing the queen
drunk as it takes
dancing
typewriter keys

compensating

eyes dissolving
like alka-seltzers

ms prissy

she hadn't worked there long
but found it all agreeable enough
tying these guys up   or spanking them
dressing them in dresses
pissing on this one character
it's not a rough place   and the money's good
but she got a call from her daddy last night
and he's really changed
and he wants her home with him   she shudders
the thoughts them nights of cold breath
be quiet baby be quiet
she's locking the cuffs   his spreadeagled guilt
and lost to herself   this fool at her mercy
she's thinking   yes daddy   i'll do it
as she's teasing his prick
and she's teasing her own mind too
and he's a godalmighty mary
and she's squeezing his nuts
oh goddamn   he whimpers and moans
she lets go   her daddy's rubbing
her raw little nipples   she leans over his face
and she plays with her lipstick   then licking
him all over his face   across his mouth
before he can move   or think
and his cock's like a geiger-counter
she's thinking him beating her mother
how many years ago was that?
and what does it matter now?

he's begging her   mary   what's wrong with you?
as she picks up the roll of saran wrap
and starts to wrap it around his face
around and around until it's all gone
forever and ever amen

small sacrifice

he steps down
the steep swirling
two by sixes
nailed
haphazardly
the back way down
to the hallway
carpet wet
sticky
filth
he steps through
the peeling layers
particle board
door loose
the hinges
the dim cubicle
the glass
the back wall
the curtain
the buzzer
he pushes
she peeks
and laughs when
she recognizes
him and pushes
the curtains aside
he drops his
quarters the slot

the glass rises
half   she's
smoking her
wet lips   leave
red smears
the white filter
"you could tie me up"
he tells her
unzipping
and dropping
his trousers
to his knees
"i'll pay you
whatever you want you
can do whatever
you want to me   take
it out on me
all them filthy bastards
ever hit you   hurt you
you could hit me
hurt me   all them big
strong wonderful men
you worship
i worship
i never was
you could even
kill me . . ."

the bondage model

i have a fantasy
i'm a woman   all suffering
and sensual
and ready to be used
like tammy wynette   and soap operas
bruised
bloody
blonde
heart
pounding
buddy rich   licks
wedding satin
cocoon
hold like corset stay
or master say so
cinched   erotic pinch
manners and artifice
like discipline
and boundaries
celebrating
sacrifice and surrender
i am fantasy
hostage/
suffocating
body/
fingers
struggling knots/
frustrated

entertainment men
worshipped/envied
feared
and hated/ more
than i have ever
felt
or been

the live peep-show

standing on tip-toes
2 o'clock angle

poking the glass hole
milking machine

her hand stops
the light goes out

she's squeezing
and stroking it/sick sweet
smell of
baby oil
(just so long
as that light is on)

i try to pretend that
we're human too
but that's not what we're
here to do

she won't even
look at me

i'm one
like lots

cum

and like
that
it's over

filling out the report

morning's your skull's nervous tic
the reason the ransom
comes home to roost

night's sawed off spew
dripping the walls
this woman's drugs
another's attitude
the politics
of when and where
and which one
leaves you laughing

(nothing holy
or lasting about
any of them
you promise yourself)

she's modern enough to show you
the door swings both ways
propping open your legs
(talked you out of your hands)
spread-eagled face-down
hunching the satin

stripped your wallet
cash and cards
and your lust

became a rubber hose
turned out the lights
and beat you
senseless

i drop in the turf last friday night

black leather
cycle cat
right there in the door

"get your name on my dick"
he sneers

i'm thinking
"aw fuck"

"come here"
he says
"where we can
see each other

look at this" laughing
flicking his lighter
pull his lower
lip
down

"fuck you"
stitched there
whack me on the chest
3 cop cars

pulling up
outside   he don't

give a fuck   pulls out
his cock
"your name" tattooed

and an "x" he's howling
and pounding his empty beer
bottle on the bar

and he's wacky on something
and raring to go
slings me

off to the side
as the cops come
storming

the bust

cops at
the door curt
boots it
one last time
slips the needle out
presses the vein
a greasy dish towel
cops pounding harder
i got my shirt
sleeves rolled
answering the door
and the questions
no problem
asking about michael
and he's my friend
i say sure
another junkie
pulled a service
station job
last night and i'd
been seen with him
"sure i gave him
a goddamn ride" and
i'm sweating my rush
and these cops know
blood trickling
down my arm

"officer i got to
sit down" i tell him
and do   on the porch
curt inside
hyperventilating
peter   his friend
in the corner
his spike still
in his arm   as good
as dead   officer says
"you mind we look
inside?"

the survival-reality game

i hear them all out there
screaming and hollering
screaming and hollering
i ain't gonna peek
or unlock

or pull that bolt
let em all in the shelter
like noah's neighbors
they been jeering years
ignoring everything i said
play me for a fool instead
fuck them motherfuckers
i stood my door and said
and then went on back in
my head

how the dark clouds
pour out pornography
what is pornography
but hope gone dry
one last try
some of that good old-fashioned
guilt coming true
on the paper
so i don't have to suffer
i don't have to really risk it/live it
be exposed

somebody see me
what i am

i hear them all out there
the demons and the doubters
tearing at their faces
building bombs/passing laws
pawing the dust applause
my heathen soul some
ne'er do well or
king of the corp
because there ain't no difference
way men are anymore
(the walls and the furniture
shivering/breathing
nothing on the radio
all the mirrors turn green
i'm capt survivor
good hard cock
in hand joystick
captain courageous
evade the last
illusion

fuck the weak
and the simple

drive that
mercy
home

i make friends everywhere i go

i'm drinking since noon sunday
i'm nuts it's hot and the kid's
every step i turn
we go to the bar
i'll shoot him the front table
little cutie comes up wants to know
can she beat him up take his cue
i'm looking like what
and shaking my head   later   vandy   blondie
drinking like she never does
back up in my face some shit i tell her
to bite one   and she spits in my face
i slap her hard reflex reaction
she can't fucking believe it
her friends realize she's ridiculous
and pull her outside
marsha says   glad you're taking
it out on her   later on
blonde back even drunker   slurring
how she's never been slapped before
but her eyes almost   sparkling

the outlaw legend/how it dies

pee wee gaskins
starring in the circus called
south carolina

1 o'clock in the morning
we're all here to party

"i believe in that eye for an eye crap"
jimmy tells the tv reporter

pee wee gaskins
the first white con
nearly half a century
gonna fry
for offing
a nigger

with a bomb he made
in prison
"i'm no racist"
he smiles
"i just think people belong
where they belong"

he can swallow
and hold
a razor blade
his esophagus

spit it up
slit

his wrists   they can
stitch him up
bind him with gauze
bed guard rails
he's all better
the state can
kill him proper

and there's a mess of us out there
in the ugly southern night
something to do
pee wee gaskins

"he's a fucking legend   man!"
driving around florence county
in his uncle's old hearse
at the age of 13
he hit his cousin in the head
with an ax and
left her for dead

he drowned a pregnant woman
and her two year old baby
because the father was black

he lived his own code

served coca-cola
and rat poison

to a woman
who'd given drugs
to his niece
and her friend

though he'd already killed
both of them by then

was convicted for 9 murders
confessed to 15
denied 10 of them at the end
too many witnesses
seen everything

"barbeque the motherfucker!"
people are chanting
euphoria clawing to a peak
bars all over columbia
throwing pee wee parties
it's a thursday night
everybody looking
something to do

middle of the woods
middle of the night
crowd like that steam   rock   hiss
swaying back and forth song

"na na na na
hey hey hey
good bye"

pee wee gaskins
they strapped his ass down

tripped the switch
let the current ride

his balls explode
his eyes
bulging blood
bursting his veins
pee wee's laughter
all that's left us
death

no more now
than it ever was
his mind/
his lips

connie learns the tricks

it was the first time
she worked the south side
and not that many nights
beyond doing it a dancer
kind of a tip
and this guy's head of his company
from south carolina
and up in his room she's sucking him
he's smashing her face ramming her
choking her she gags and her teeth raking
him he goes crazy his fist shatters
her cheek her temple
splinters and stars
and he half picks her up
slaps and slings the bed
she don't know where she is
and he's got the rope ready
secures her the headboard
calls his buddies in
from the convention
tells them she's paid to enjoy it
they rape all night next morning
it's the whiskey thing they pour
a half pint down her throat
got her half-dressed coming through
the lobby the liquor hits
there's a lot of winking
and folded bills

they all see him slip
a fistful of bills
her purse and a big one
the cabby saying hey how about
taking her somewhere uptown
you know she was a real good time.

i ain't retarded but. . .

              sure   they call me names
tease me   pick on me   down at the docks
              we unload the trains
       sweating greasy hot slut afternoon
       "you ever had a woman shitface?"
        "you suck your own" i tell him
           i don't take nothing
              none of them
       and i know what's going on
        what people think of me
   that was the hard part   all my life
i knew women   thought me ugly   pretty women
  laughing at me   behind my back   in my face

     and i live down at the merchant's
and i don't have no woman come stay with me
    i lay there   i'm a man   i've got urges
      rubbing it sometimes   normal urges
        but i ain't got no woman
i'm watching the news this abortion center
    they're protesting and screeching
     and some of the girls are
     crying and hiding their faces
  this blonde haired thin lipped lady
handing out baby dolls and birthday cards
    "you're murderers" she's shrieking
   and shaking her manicured fist
     and i'm thinking about it

maybe stalking
this crazy bitch
grabbing her   raping her
over and over   saying
i'm going to do this until
i'm sure you're pregnant
(ugly is as ugly does—
and i've already told you
how ugly i was)

like i'd tell her
i'm so ugly
i shoulda never
been born

cassie cops a feeling

out on dickerson road
talking playing
the make-up
strutting her
5-inch heels
"sure i feel sorry
some of them" she's telling
the 6 o'clock cameras
the men she's caught
this police sting
"but i don't feel sorry
the AIDS they're taking home
killing their wives and kids"
she's a smug smile
on a clown face
fat red lips pinwheel whorls her cheeks
"my old lady ain't fucked me in 10 years"
pathetic little fellow
shouting over the hallowed
pronouncements the reporter
seems he's preaching
his sunday school lesson
so sincere his outrage
the sin in our fair city
cassie's tits riding
over her push-up
she's still breathing hard
some slams this skinny guy

against the car and cuff him
re-enactment 3rd take
"it's like playing a role"
she's telling the camera
chewing her gum
smacking it
twirling her lipstick
up and down nervously
and smiling   "i love you
lady cop"   the little fellow
squirming the back seat
the squad car

scars so quiet

out in the field
four of em

broke him down
that night

stretched and held
him flexing

manhood
ugly shadows
twisting
cloudy

lips 'n moon
she lays there
can't move

his screams like
razors cross her face

he's vacant
quiet
now

stares and scowls
like she ain't there

she wants him back
he's gone
forever

harry suggs

so what about harry
he's one gentle joyous soul
always got his hat
a crumpled '40s fedora
and his clothes kinda hanging
skinny and hollow in the hold
his drugs all the time wasted drunk
and stoned pot open and free about it
the psychedelics too he's got 'em
and a little too wide open common sense
as we moved into the '80s
and barred from the place
one of its heydays
and walking up that hot august
we're all out there on that cement porch
and he's got his harp and we end up
"amazing grace" his old standby
and a bunch of the others
he was a regular i ran
the writer's nights down here
and any number weekend bands
especially dave and pat
he was mr party drugs and dancing
and feeling good that's what
he stood for and a harmless man
if a simple one and kay came out there
ran him off and he walked off on up
the alley it was 7 or so and just

getting long in the shadows

and the next day was sunday
we were driving back down there
talking about the copper wire bracelets
he'd made and given us there on the dashboard
simple swirls cut from a spool
with needle-nosed pliers harry's new venture
and we got down there and heard how
some fellow everyone described
looking like a rat or something kicked him
to death up the alley late
and there were some stood around and watched it
and never said nothing
and harry was a small man
and drunk and helpless
and harry was black and surrounded by
white faces and most of them knew him
and he never done anything against any of them
and he didn't deserve dying that way

the white man

has worshipped waste

and taught god greed

he has altered nature

to satisfy whim and comfort

he has closed in on himself

for so long

and so well

when he dies

the whole world

rises as one

politics & pornography

marge piercy
jesse helms

the organic left &
the christian soldiers
predict their computers

share everyone
certain virtues/
instincts

x & y means so & so
sees it all
same way i do
you do
we all do
don't you?

dignity
integrity
desire
& intentions
can be measured
graphically

the standards   a community
a nation   a world
reality's mirror

america's successfully
polished appearance
locking the door

here we are and there are
none live up to
the lust that is us

for family and friends
and self   so well-defined
the corridors
the brimstone

feminists
vegetarians
& skinheads
republicans
tin cans
democrats
& dogshit

2 parties mean
only game in town
is rigged
under the rugged
cross of our
hotheaded blood

o america

with the holy hand
of god in marriage

thy makest me
to lie down
in strange beds

this porno shop

exploits women sure it does
a good fourth of the wall racks
gay shit/ a good 70% the clientele
going for a blow job or a quick hand
the glory holes between the quarter
video booths — a fifth of the store
swinger/contact rip-off mags
some of the ads 20 years old
high percentage whore/masseuse/
model/escorts offering glorified
jack jobs cost you up to a hundred
you that timid or stupid
there's the bondage/tv/female domination
corner too the fetishes/rubber & leather wear
and there's the dildos/the cock rings/
the inflatable dolls   exploits women?   sure
and shames men the silliness our society
drives to these base levels
can't look you in the eye
ashamed to talk about it
(except the gays of course
who realized a long time ago
the abuse comes with the freedom—)
it's something the exploited
middle-class american heterosexual
frustratedly sits and fantasizes
& filth is where you see it

ted bundy's mother

she's an older pious orthodox   mormon i suppose
though she could be baptist catholic jewish

mother's devotion
and is it comforting to think

pictures in magazines
make him hop about

some external evil
perverted
the christian love

more than the caricature
the traditional values

he was a good boy   she says   a tremble in her voice
but her head held   high

sex was never mentioned
i don't understand

he didn't learn any of this around here

she really doesn't
understand
and she just wishes
you would all
go away

good kids

they were good kids
went to the best schools
got anything they wanted
all the breaks

and bored
beat in the head
of a guy i knew
for 63 bucks
outside a bar where he worked
for less than minimum wage

for kicks
one of a hundred or so "jobs"
kept them kicking that summer
crashed car
september joyride
cops came and took them away

papa posted bond
immediately/ tied it up
all winter
backrooms and favors

and the judge couldn't see
how justice would be served
next spring when
court costs

allowances
and fall tuitions

came from the same wallet
and they spent that summer
planting trees out
percy priest lake
community service

repast

I offended my eyes and plucked them
tore the tongue from the mouth
that mocked me

unscrewed the bulb
and sat there
without blinking

while the blisters scabbed over
and as I needed neither
pain nor any of its prerequisites
to spur me

I hung my hands
like retired guns
on wooden pegs

sent my feet
like children
to bed

and waited all night
for the warning buzzer
alarm and scream

the hysterical flip of the spatula
and morning

a bulging yellow eye
a crusty ridge of brown curled lips
cussing
spitting

tasteless
(if that still matters)
I'm finally hot enough
to serve you

exactly what was called for
a long long time ago

the boll weevil blues

15-20 of 'em   came from the church
a couple carried rifles
one of 'em a shotgun
we'd been camping the river
for a couple of weeks
talking earlier 'bout heading toward texas
and some of 'em wearing
masks and hoods
and they strapped
his arms to his sides with a belt
then they beat him and kicked him
and he bled and he jerked and he twitched
then he felt nothing at all he was dead
the sonuvabitch   he fucked my sister
the only thing he said to me
then two of 'em grabbed me
this is just so you don't remember
nothing wrong huh mister?
got the boll weevil blues everywhere i ever been
the boll weevil blues   everywhere i ever been
i just didn't fit in   never went back again

Acknowledgments

Some poems in this collection have been published previously in various journals and magazines. Grateful acknowledgment is made to the following publications:

AIM (American Intercultural Magazine); *alph null*; *angelflesh*; *APA EROS*; *Atom Mind*; *the back alley review*; *The Baltimore Sun*; *Barbeque Planet*; *Bogg*; *Buckle*; *Burning World*; *Contact II*; *Calliope's Corner*; *Clock Radio*; *Coke Fish*; *crawlspace*; *The Dekalb Literary Arts Journal*; *Dog River Review*; *Dreams & Nightmares*; *The Drowning World*; *En Passant/etc*; *Face the Demon*; *Format*; *Four I's*; *The Fisk Herald*; *Ginger Hill*; *A Good Day to Die*; *Gypsy*; *Hollow Spring Review*; *Howling Dog*; *IDOMO*; *Impulse*; *jukebox terrorists with typewriters*; *Kameleon*; *Kindred Spirits*; *Lactuca*; *MAAT*; *Maelstrom Review*; *Mamashee*; *mysterious wysteria*; *Nashville Poetry Anthology*; *occasional review*; *Open 24 Hours*; *Passaic Review*; *The Pawn Review*; *The Penny Dreadful Review*; *persona non grata chapbooks*; *The Pikestaff Forum*; *pinched nerve*; *The Pinchpenny Review*; *The Plastic Tower*; *Pluma True Review*; *Poetry Motel*; *Public Property*; *The Remington Review*; *River Rat Review*; *roadhouse*; *raw bone*; *Samisdat*; *smiling dog press*; *Something We Can't Name* (anthology); *Windows on the Cumberland: Readings 1984-1994*; *scree*; *Slipstream*; *Tandava*; *Taurus*; *Tears In The Fence*; *Truly Fine Press*; *Vagabond's House*; *Versus*; *Visions*; *Wind*; *whoopin' it up in nashville tn*; *Yellow Butterfly*.

About the Author

TOM HOUSE is a Nashville-based poet and singer-songwriter who has received worldwide attention for his unique recordings and performances. An independent cassette—Inside These Walls—and CD's on the Checkered Past label—*The Neighborhood is Changing* and *This White Man's Burden*—received critical acclaim and have placed him securely in the new fringe genre "Americana." Newer releases on Catamount Records—*'Til You've Seen Mine*, *Jesus Doesn't Live Here Anymore*, and *Long Time Home From Here*—continue to receive praise and acknowledgement. Tom also serves as the long-time driving spirit behind the Working Stiffs Jambouree, a Nashville institution that features eclectic, non-mainstream talent. Tom has had over 400 poems published nationally and internationally; his poems have been translated into Italian, German, French, and Japanese. Earliest publications include the *Southern Poetry Review*, the *Duke Archive*, and the *St. Andrew's Review*. Later work found its place with Road House Press and magazines like *Bogg*, *nausea*, and *Poetry Motel*. In 1996, The *Tennessee Bi-Centennial Anthology* feautured three of Tom's poems. Tom has had numerous chapbooks put out by various small-press publishers and has put out others on his own. Tom states that his poetry has a "rough" edge that "remains true to the character and situation of the narrative." Tom works on his songwriting and poetry with equal passion and commitment, as he believes "songwriting can truly be poetry in its own stead."